WHAT'S INSIDE A Drone?

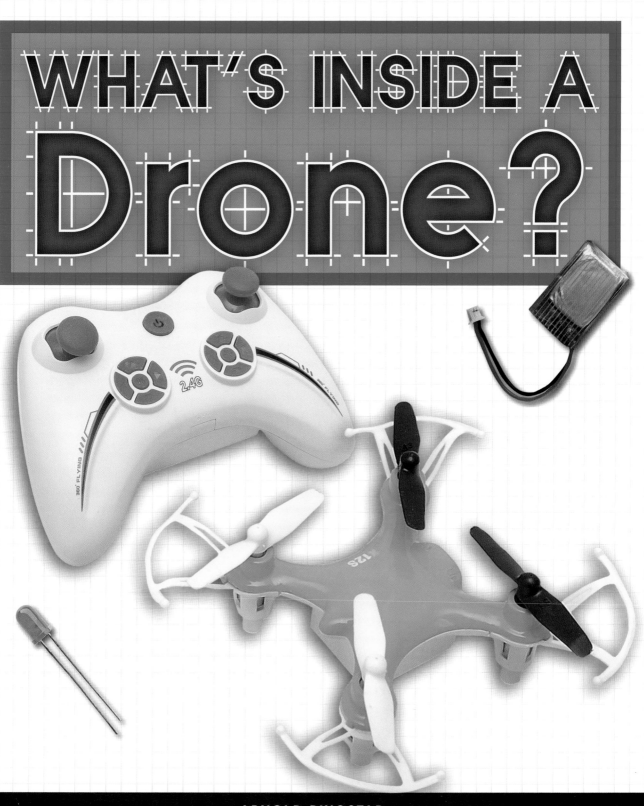

ARNOLD RINGSTAD

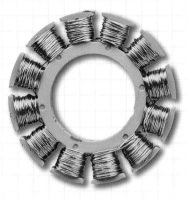

The Child's World®
childsworld.com

Published by The Child's World®
1980 Lookout Drive • Mankato, MN 56003-1705
800-599-READ • www.childsworld.com

Photographs ©: Rick Orndorf, cover (drone), cover (controller), 1 (drone), 1 (controller), 4 (controller), 4 (drone), 7, 9, 10 (joystick), 11, 13, 14 (antenna), 16, 17 (top), 17 (bottom), 19 (top), 19 (bottom), 20 (joystick), 23 (propeller), 24; Shutterstock Images, cover (bulb), 1 (bulb), 2, 3 (plug), 3 (circuit board), 5 (glasses), 6 (bulb), 8 (screw), 8 (circuit board), 10 (circuit board), 12, 15, 18 (bulb), 20 (buttons), 23 (circuit board); Pedro Sala/Shutterstock Images, cover (battery), 1 (battery), 6 (battery); Praiwun Thungsarn/Shutterstock Images, 3 (screwdriver), 5 (screwdriver), 14 (screwdriver); Shyripa Alexandr/ Shutterstock Images, 5 (gloves); Oleksandr Kostiuchenko/Shutterstock Images, 18 (battery), 21

ISBN 9781503832374
LCCN 2018963100

Printed in the United States of America
PA02419

About the Author

Arnold Ringstad lives in Minnesota.

He enjoys flying drones with his friends.

Contents

Materials and Safety

Materials

- [ ] Drone
- [ ] Phillips screwdriver
- [ ] Safety glasses
- [ ] Work gloves

Safety

- Be careful when handling sharp objects, such as screwdrivers.

- Wear work gloves to protect your hands from sharp edges.

- Wear safety glasses in case pieces snap off.

Drone

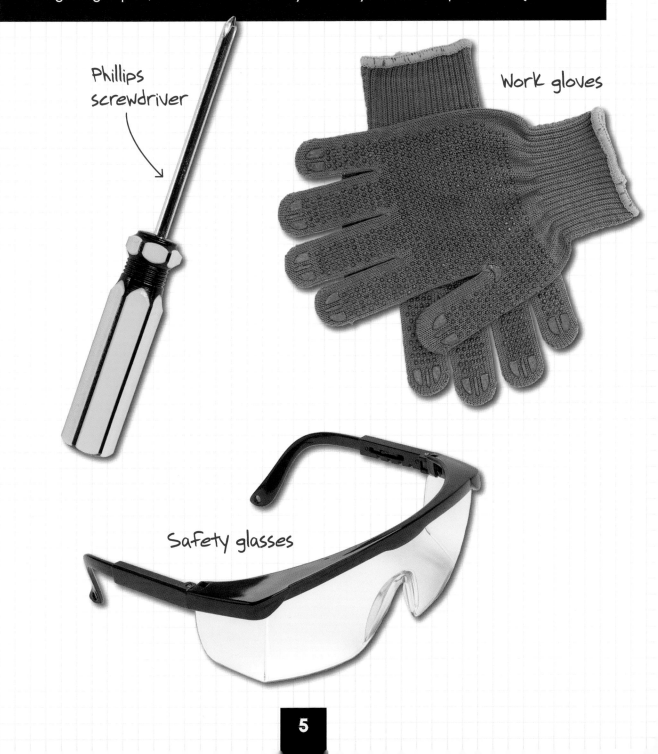

Phillips screwdriver

Work gloves

Safety glasses

Inside a Drone

Many people enjoy flying drones.
These flying machines can rise high
into the air. They can zoom around
quickly. They can even hover in
place. How do drones work?
What's inside?

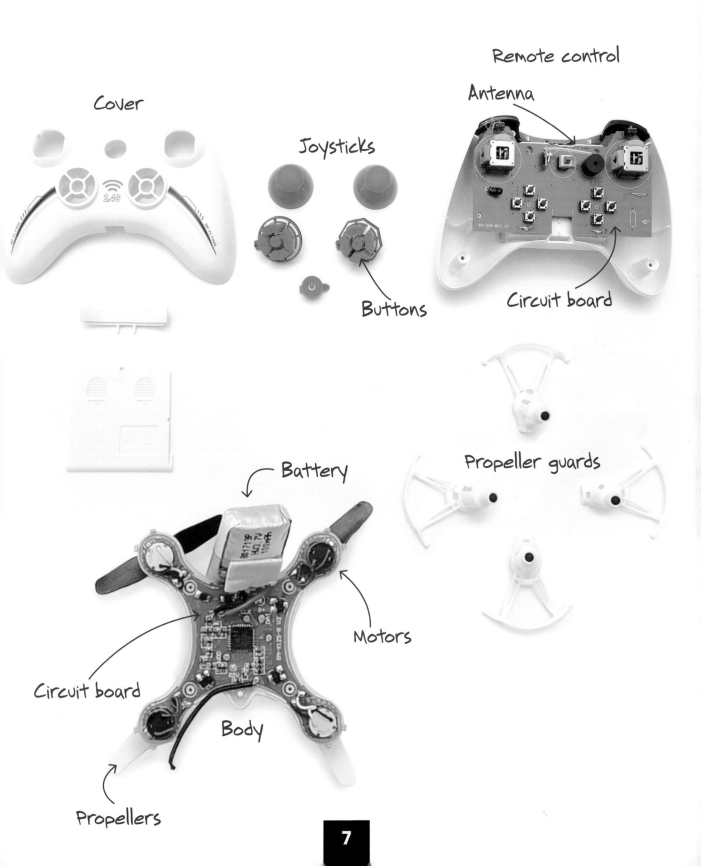

Cover

Joysticks

Remote control

Antenna

Buttons

Circuit board

Battery

Propeller guards

Motors

Circuit board

Body

Propellers

Opening the Drone

Tiny screws hold the drone's body together. Unscrew them. Then pull the pieces of the body apart. Inside you can see the battery. Pull the battery away to see the **circuit board** underneath.

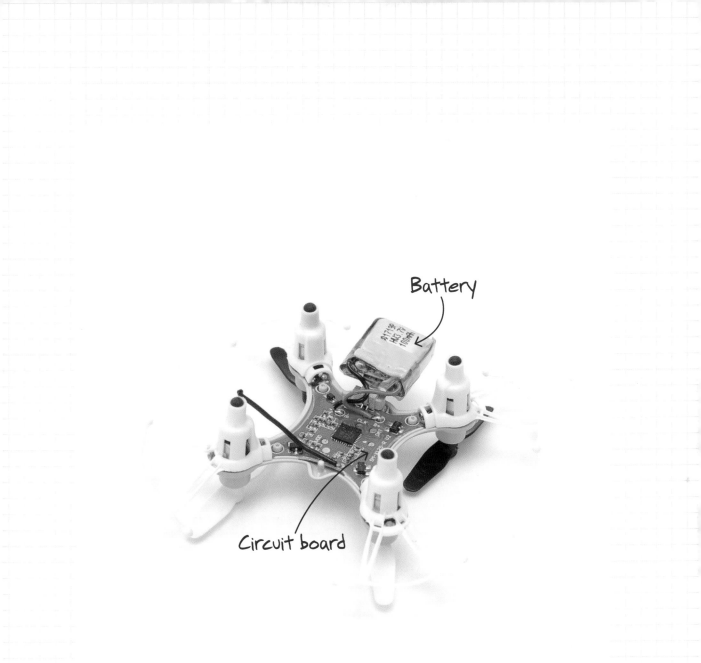

Battery

Circuit board

A small circuit board fills most of the drone's body.

Inside the Remote Control

Screws hold the remote control together. Remove them to open it up. Inside you can see a circuit board, buttons, and **joysticks**.

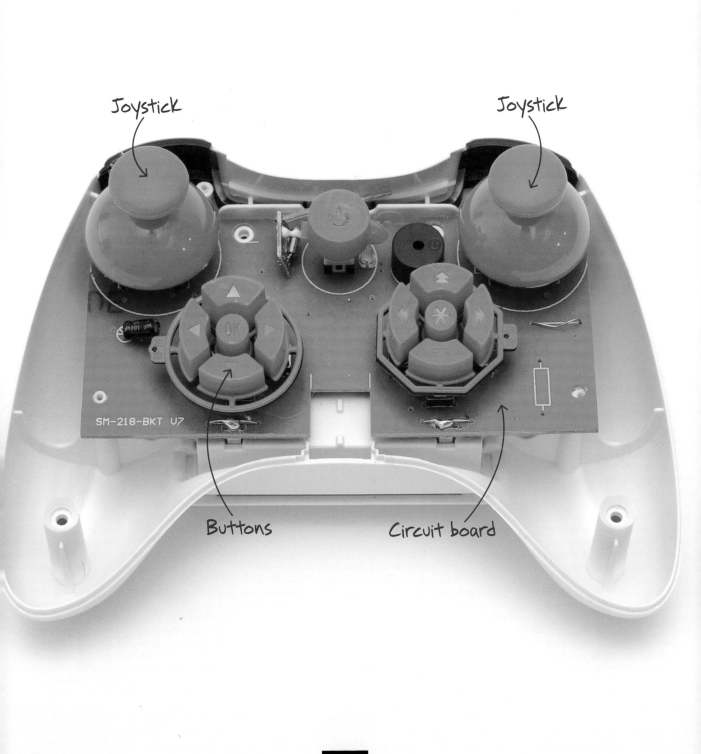

Joystick

Joystick

Buttons

Circuit board

SM-218-BKT V7

Sending Signals

The user pushes buttons and moves joysticks on the remote control. The remote control's circuit board turns these instructions into electrical **signals**. It uses an **antenna** to send these signals to the drone.

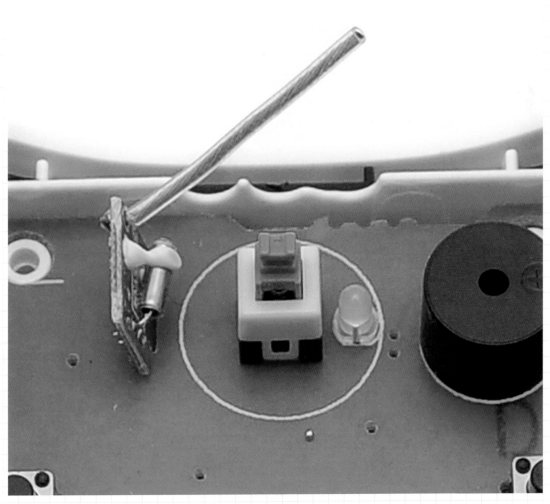

The small antenna sticks out of the circuit board.

Receiving Signals

The drone receives the signals
with its own antenna. A **microchip**
processes the signals.

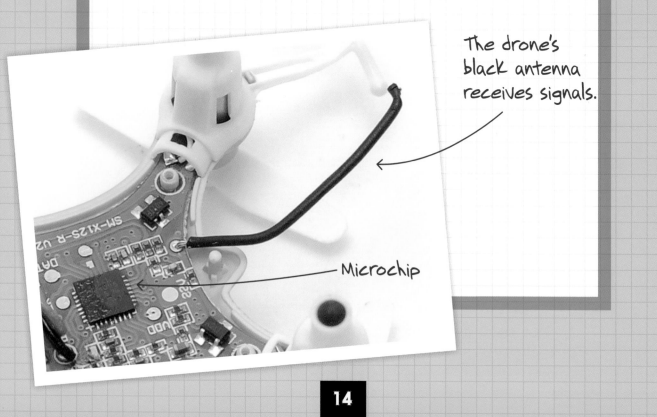

The drone's
black antenna
receives signals.

Microchip

The microchip figures out how fast the **motors** need to spin. Each motor is attached to a **propeller**. To fly up, all four propellers go fast. To fly forward, the front propellers slow down and the rear ones speed up. To hover, they all spin at a steady speed.

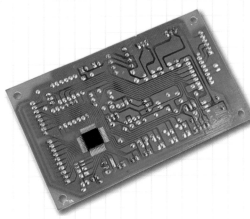

Propeller Guards

The propellers are protected by propeller guards. These plastic pieces stop the drone from getting damaged if it crashes. Pull the propeller guards away. Underneath you can see the motors.

The drone has two white propellers and two black propellers.

Flying with Motors

Power is stored in the drone's battery. From the battery, power flows into the circuit board. There, the microchip decides how fast each motor needs to spin. It sends power to the motors. The microchip carefully controls the motors to follow the user's instructions.

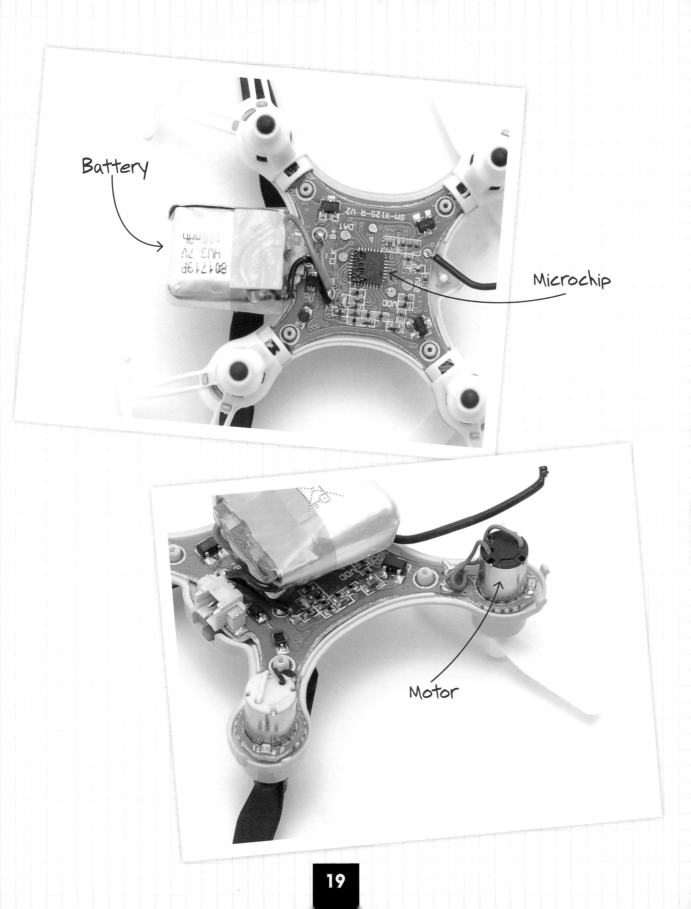

Battery

Microchip

Motor

Reusing a Drone

We've taken apart a drone and learned what's inside. Now what? Here are some ideas for how to reuse the parts of a drone. Can you think of any more?

- **A Better Drone**: Think of ways you could change the drone. What if the battery were larger or smaller? What if the motors were bigger? How would the drone fly differently?

- **Gaming Controller**: The remote control is similar to video game controllers. Compare the drone remote to a game controller. What parts do they share?

Glossary

antenna (an-TEN-uh): An antenna is a wire that sends or receives signals. An antenna in the remote control sends signals.

circuit board (SUR-kit BORD): A circuit board is a piece of material that holds computer chips, switches, and other parts. The drone and the remote control each contain a circuit board.

joysticks (JOY-stiks): Joysticks are parts of controllers that let the user steer in a direction. Moving the joysticks steers the drone.

microchip (MY-kroh-chip): A microchip is a part that contains electrical circuits designed to do a certain job. In the drone, a microchip helps control the motors.

motors (MOH-turz): Motors are the parts of machines that create motion. The drone's four motors let it fly.

propeller (pruh-PEL-ur): A propeller is a part that spins to help push objects in a certain direction. Each motor in the drone has its own propeller.

signals (SIG-nuhlz) Signals are electrical pulses sent through antennas. The remote control sends signals to the drone.

To Learn More

IN THE LIBRARY

Hustad, Douglas. *Discover Drones*. Minneapolis, MN: Lerner Publications, 2017.

Marsico, Katie. *Drones*. New York, NY: Children's Press, 2016.

Ringstad, Arnold. *What's Inside a Remote-Controlled Car?* Mankato, MN: The Child's World, 2020.

ON THE WEB

Visit our website for links about taking apart a drone: **childsworld.com/links**

Note to Parents, Teachers, and Librarians: We routinely verify our Web links to make sure they are safe and active sites. So encourage your readers to check them out!

Index